An Anglo-Indian Childhood

by
Shirley Gifford-Pritchard

authorHOUSE™

1663 LIBERTY DRIVE, SUITE 200
BLOOMINGTON, INDIANA 47403
(800) 839-8640
WWW.AUTHORHOUSE.COM

© *2005 Shirley Gifford-Pritchard. All Rights Reserved.*

No part of this book may be reproduced, stored in a retrieval system, or transmitted by any means without the written permission of the author.

First published by AuthorHouse 10/26/05

ISBN: 1-4208-8663-0 (sc)

Printed in the United States of America
Bloomington, Indiana

This book is printed on acid-free paper.

This book is dedicated to my two children, Christina and Mark, and to my husband, Brian, with all my love.

Besides its being a history of my family in India, another reason for writing this book is that in this, the 21st century, the Anglo-Indian community will have been absorbed through marriage into the other cultures to which they emigrated and our little ethnic group will soon disappear from this world in peoples' consciousness and in actuality.

A special "shukria" (thank you) to Brian for his infinite patience and technical help. When I became frustrated and bad-tempered, he would use the Anglo-Indian expression "Wait on, wait on", complete with accent, which would make me laugh and get me back on track.

Shirley

Author as happy baby

DORSEY-GIFFORD FAMILY TREE

John Alcock (Gifford) m. Ellen Maloney *Arthur Francis Dorsey m. Rosamond Adelaide Holt*
1921-1921 *1858-1924*

| |

George Harrington Alcock Gifford m. Mary Smith *Ernest Dorsey m. Margaret Rose Coshan*
1860-1909 *1861-1913* *1885-1950* *1890-1963*

| |

Annie William Minnie Lily Lucy Alice *Lillian Melita Thelma George*
Richard Lydia Albert Amy Walter Dorothy *1912-2003 1915-1936 1918-2003 1920-2002*

Walter Gilbert Gifford m. Lilian Mary Dorsey
1985-1985 *1912-2003*

|

Shirley Mary Melita Gifford m. Brian Frederick Pritchard Moyra Margaret m. Brian O'Loughlin Patricia Mary m. Louis Kirk
1935- *1935-* *1940-* *1939-1993* *1950-* *1943-*

| |

Christina Louise *Mark Gifford* *Tara Noreen* *Darren Gifford*
1962- *1964-* *1967-* *1971-*

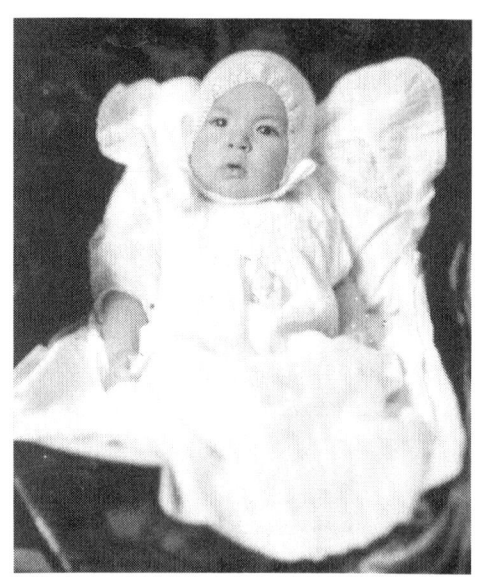

Author, born November 3, 1935

PREFACE

For those not familiar with the term "Anglo-Indian", it originally defined the off-spring of an English father and an Indian mother during the period of the British Raj in India……..but, as with all things human, there were numerous variations on the theme.

"Eurasian" would probably have been a more accurate term as French, Portuguese and other European bloodlines were also involved in the occupation of the sub-continent. (The Portuguese with Goa on the west coast by the Arabian Sea and the French in Pondicherry on the east coast by the Bay of Bengal). However, the term Eurasian carried its own prejudices against slant-eyed foreigners during that era and so the term "Anglo-Indian" was favored.

Also, the Anglo-Indians wished to separate themselves from the Goans who were Indians christened by the Portuguese missionaries and given Christian names like Mary and Joseph followed by surnames like Fernandes or Rodriques. In an attempt to gain cachet with the ruling class, some Goans would change their names from Fernandes to the more English-sounding Fern, from Rodrigues to Rodricks or Meneses to Menzies, to site just a few examples. Sometimes it was an outright change to an English name with no resemblance to the former one. There was usually no mixed blood except in an occasional liaison between a Portuguese man and an Indian woman.

It was quite usual in mixed marriages between Europeans and Indians to have a pale-skinned child with light hair and eyes and a sibling with darker skin, black hair and brown eyes …. and variations therein.

The English who were born and lived in India chose the term "Domiciled European" to distance themselves from anyone who might possibly carry mixed blood. The ruling party was British and white and that was the ideal culture aspired to in form and speech and manners in order to attain both social acceptance and professional gain. Resultantly, the word "fair" (meaning fair-skinned) became the most prized and complimentary word used when describing a person – and persists even in today's India.

What follows is a personal recollection of a time in India long past when there was no doubt that God was an Englishman and an era the likes of which would never be seen again - for better or worse. In a way, it is my mother who should have written this book as she could recount many more stories of British India than I.

To illustrate how culturally indoctrinated they were, when my mother went to school, the second language taught was French (as in any British school in the United Kingdom). Being taught Hindi was not even considered. However, by the time I came along, India was well on it's way to independence. This took place in 1947 when I was 12 years old and the second language then became mandatory Hindi and which we learned somewhat resentfully.

With the advent of Independence, the Raj disappeared almost overnight. The English departed en masse for home leaving the Anglo-Indians very lost. Although culturally

English, the vast majority had never been to England and yet were jeered at by the newly independent Indian to "Go Home". For my parents' generation, this was a hard choice; to leave the land of their birth and a lifestyle that could not be duplicated for the cold clime of England.

But that's another story....

Walter Gifford & Lilian Dorsey on their wedding day

Uncle George, Granddad, Granny, Dad, Mum, Thelma, Ozzie Kelly (Melita's husband) & Melita

ANCESTRY

India, the Jewel and the Crown of the British Empire. My parents were born in this romantic country of the Moguls, of Kipling, of tales of the Northwest Frontier, of the fabulous Taj Mahal, of stunning architecture, of colorful saris... and Kashmir, so beautiful and desirable that men, to this day, are dying to possess her.

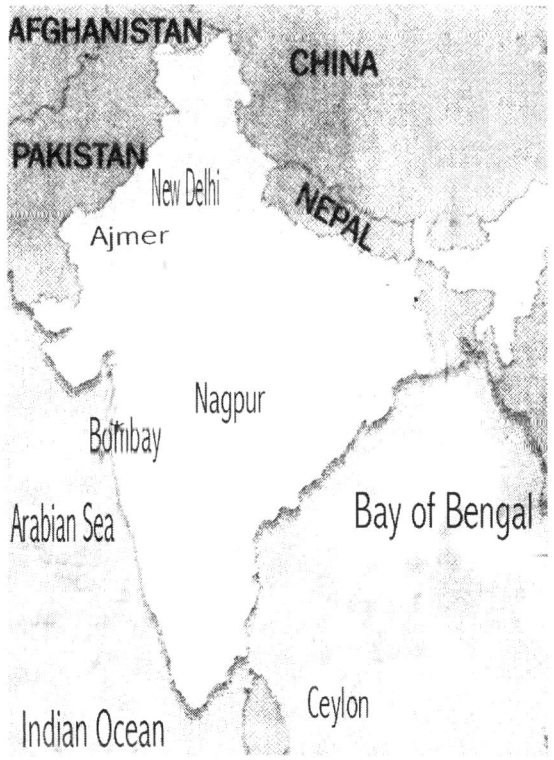

The magnificent Himalayas feed the great Brahmaputra River which, in turn, connects with the holy Ganges and spills into the Bay of Bengal through her fertile delta. In the west, the mountains sweep down to the plains and the River Indus with her tributaries, the Jeelub, Chenab, Ravi, Bias and Sutlege, flow into the Arabian Sea.

Further south is the Ran of Kutch and then the sub-continent slowly contracts, past the Tropic of Cancer, till her tip ends, separated by the sparkling Indian Ocean from a pear-shaped droplet which is Ceylon (now Sri Lanka).

My father, Walter Gilbert Gifford, was born on a plantation in the Nilgiri Hills in Southern India. His father, George Harrington Alcock, was an Englishman who, for property reasons, legally changed his name to Gifford.

Paternal Grandfather George Harrington (Alcock) Gifford

He came out to British India, the Jewel in the Crown, in the late 1800s to plant tea. He married a Mary Smith about whom we know very little. It is suspected that the reason for this could be ignorance or outright subterfuge as she might have been Indian or, at the very least, mixed.

The family also seems to have been ostracized by the "proper" English community and, eventually, George's brother, who had married a Lady North with evidently the "right" connections, wrested the estate from the family.

Dad's parents died at a fairly young age and the eight daughters and four sons, after being schooled by the nuns and priests in Ootacamund (or "Ootie" as it is affectionately called) and Coonor, eventually scattered throughout India.

My father became a Training Instructor in the Post & Telegraphs – an individual much-loved by his students and all who met him. A gentleman and a gentle man. When he lost his temper (which was rare), the strongest expression we ever heard from him was, "Dash it all".

Anglo-Indians were given preference in the areas of Telegraphs, Railways, Civil Service and the Army. This was done not due to any particular affection but because it made practical sense; the A-I's were culturally British with no language barriers and were useful as a buffer between the ruling English and subjugated Indians.

Ernest with three-year old Lilian & Maggie with Baby Melita

My mother, Lilian Dorsey, was born in Chapra, in the shadow of the mighty Himalayas, a small town in Bhopal State in the northeast of India. Chapra was later razed by an earthquake.

Her father was Ernest Patrick Dorsey of Irish descent and her mother, Margaret Coshan was part-French.

Ernest Dorsey was also employed by the Post & Telegraphs. He was the brother of Mervyn Dorsey, the father of the singer Arnold Dorsey, better known as Engelbert Humperdinck, my cousin and the family's only claim to fame – so far!

Ernest and Maggie had three girls and one boy. Lilian, my mother, Melita (who tragically died in her twenties shortly after her honeymoon), Thelma and George.

Lilian, Thelma & Melita

My parents had 4 girls, all spaced evenly 5 years apart. Myself, Shirley Mary Melita, the oldest, then Moyra Margaret Mary, followed by Anne Marie (who died two days after birth) and Patricia Mary who, much to her disgust was nicknamed Paddy May. *(Years later when she emigrated to the United States, she embraced the opportunity to change it forever to Tricia!)*

The story goes that the photographer had trouble keeping me still until he found a book with doggie pictures.

Moyra, five years my junior, was, in the sibling hierarchy of such things, considered by me a pest but by my mother as a necessary appendage whenever I went out to play. There her presence made me appreciate her even less as she is and has always been her own person and, therefore, not necessarily constricted by social custom. To explain: when we played "Hide & Go Seek" at some point or the other one has to be "It"….well, Moyra would play along till it was her turn to be "It" then breezily declare "I'm going home – I don't want to play anymore" while I, burdened with a nature that wants to please everyone, would die of embarrassment .

This difference in our natures was also manifest in the way we reacted to punishment. I would immediately say, "Sorry, sorry" and burst into tears. Moyra on the other hand, as young as she was, would defiantly refuse to apologize and would then be put in the corner, where she would pick at the "chunam" (whitewash). After 20 minutes or so, my mother would say, "Alright, you can come out now" and the little tyke would turn around and announce, "It's okay. I like it here", completely turning the tables while I watched in awe and profound admiration.

AJMER

My first recollections of childhood are of a small town called Ajmer situated on the borders of the Thar Desert in the northern state of Rajputana (now Rajasthan). It is surrounded by a range of the Aravali Hills and was strategically important to both Hindus and Muslims as there is the grave of a descendant of Mohammed on Taragarh Hill and also a holy lake called Pushka not far from Ajmer. For devotees, the gravesite substitutes for Mecca and the lake for the Ganges – subsequently, when Partition came, the fighting between the two parties was fierce.

We lived in a compound off the Srinagar Road called "Chisty Villas" and our landlord claimed to be a descendant of the Muslim buried on Taragarh Hill and, therefore, a direct descendant of Mohammed himself.

Flat-roofed house in Chisty Villas

Anglo-Indians usually rented their homes, along with some of their furniture, because they were constantly transferred and there were always Railway Quarters and Telegraph Quarters available for the staff. However, for some reason, my parents chose not to live in the Telegraph Quarters.

Chisty Villas boasted a large iron gate with a long drive, a surrounding wall and about a dozen houses within the enclave which also included servants quarters.

We spent many happy hours swinging on the big gate but my most vivid memory of the gate is of Julian D'Souza lazily trying to open it without getting out of his father's car, with the result that his arm got stuck and broken as his father obliviously drove on until he registered Julian's shriek of pain.

Most of the inhabitants of Chisty Villas were Anglo-Indians such as ourselves, the Blakes, Bristows, Barrons and D'Silvas but the family that remains excruciatingly vivid is that of Mr. & Mrs. Robbins. He was a very tall, proud Englishman and she a small, exquisite lady. He had (whether through bad luck or, even worse, his own mismanagement) lost most of his money, was losing what was left fighting in the courts, and was reduced to living in a small room and kitchen in the back of one of the houses rented from an Indian. As young as I was, I picked up from the adults how utterly mortifying this was for him and I am not sure how they were able to bear it.

One day, frail little Mrs. Robbins came over, rested her beautiful white head against our back door and said, "I think he's gone". I sneaked out the back and stole a glance at Mr. Robbins, still proud and dignified - even in death. My mother and other ladies made arrangements for poor little Mrs. Robbins to go by train to some home down in South India and I often wonder whatever happened to her. Here I will insert a short story that my mother wrote as it seems so a propos at this point:

A FRAGMENT OF MEMORY BY Lilian Gifford

"Hold on a moment, dear."

I dismounted and turned to see my husband feeling the rear tyre of his bicycle

"I hope it is only the valve and not a puncture. We'll soon find out."

While I waited, idly leaning against my bike, I glanced at the scene before me. In the near distance, range upon range of hills showed up bold and clear against the blue Rajput sky. Boulder strewn, covered with scrub and cacti, they presented a rather desolate but strangely attractive picture. In the foreground, a path meandered, losing itself after many twists and turnings in the foothills no great distance away. Loping along it at a steady trot was a "gowli" returning to his village after delivering his milk in the town of Ajmer that lay behind us, his red turban a vivid splash of colour amidst his dun-coloured surroundings. I wondered if he ever thought about, or even knew of, the many brave Rajput warriors, his ancestors, who must have trodden the same path during their gallant but vain attempts to repel the Mogul invaders from the north. Those silent, brooding hills .. what a lot they would reveal if only they could speak.

"Thank goodness it was only the valve. Now we can go on."

Turning to my husband, my mind still dwelling on the historic past, I impulsively exclaimed, "Let's not ride along our usual haunts. What about exploring a bit instead?"

"Very well. Where would you like to go?

I waved my hand in the direction of the fast disappearing milkman. My husband looked a bit doubtful.

"The roads along there are little better than sandy tracks. ..."

"We'll try it," I coaxed. "If it becomes too bad we can always turn back"

With a smile and a cheerful "Okay," my husband agreed, so we mounted and rode on. Skirting the bottom of the hill nearest us we rode along, carefully picking our way amid the ruts and sandy patches. Rounding the hill, we found ourselves near a toll gate. Beyond this stretched a road, framed on either side by tall fences made of bamboo and thorn, which my husband thought linked up with the main Jaipur Road. To the right, nestling in a hollow between two hills, was a thorpe in front of which was a garden of sorts.

Dismounting and pushing our cycles, for the path that led to the thorpe was pretty bad, we reached the garden in a few minutes and, leaning our bikes against the low stone wall, opened the gate.

Rather hesitantly we entered, wondering if we had any right to do so. A "mali" was kneeling a few feet away weeding a bed of marigolds. Approaching him we asked if we could look over the garden. Rising and salaaming politely, he gravely gave us permission to do so. It was a small garden, mostly given to the cultivation of vegetables, except for a few flower beds near the entrance and to one side. We wandered about. ...it was so quiet and peaceful.

In a far corner I suddenly noticed a grave. Whose could it be? We decided to find out. It was a rather large, simple grave, once white now a drab gray. Stooping, I tried to decipher the faded inscription, surprised to see it was in English. "To the Memory of. ..." It was a woman's name. We wondered who she was. Just then a man approached and placed a small "charak" at the head of the grave, draping a garland of jasmine beneath it. He struck a match and lit the "charak" (a tiny clay bowl filled with oil and a floating wick). We asked him why he did this and whose grave it was. All he could tell us was that she bad been an official's wife and that he had orders to place a light and some flowers on her grave each Tuesday evening. He was evidently a watchman of sorts and could add little more.

Silently we turned and made our way back. At the gate I paused and looked over my shoulder. The sun had just gone down and, in the gray tropical dusk that usually takes the place of the twilight of more northern climes, the little light shone bright and clear. Who was she ? What was the story of this Englishwoman buried many thousands of miles away from her native land in a remote and lonely pocket of the Rajput hills with only the wood pigeons to coo her requiem ? I wondered. I suppose I will never really know.

***

My mother was not only an excellent writer but loved geography and history and could make these subjects come alive. She would have made a wonderful teacher had she chosen this path.

Mum with unhappy me, Dad, Granddad, Granny, Uncle George & Aunt Thelma

Because the rainfall in Ajmer was so minimal, all the rooftops were flat and one of the loveliest recollections is of sleeping on the roof under the stars on "charpoys" (beds strung with rope on wooden legs).

The water shortage was so severe at times, that we would have to resort to well water which was brackish and did not allow the soap to lather. The precious commodity was brought on a bullock cart by the "bisthi" (water carrier) and he would empty the contents from an animal skin into our metal buckets and tin baths and get paid.

One of my fondest memories is of my beloved ayah (Indian nanny) giving me a bath and me laughingly covering her with soap while she protested, "Nyhee nyhee (no, no), Shirley Babee".

The purity of the water was constantly in question, so drinking water was always boiled, filtered through fine gauze, medicated with little red granules and deposited in "chatties" (large, porous, round, clay containers) which kept the water fairly cool.

Four generations: Mum with Baby Moyra, Great-Grandma Coshan, me and Granny Margaret Dorsey

The floors of the houses were made of stone, which could be cooled with water and the windows covered by shutters made of coconut husk, called "kus kus tatties", to both shade and cool us from the heat. To this day I can recall the wonderful smell of the wet husk.

All the houses had verandahs furnished with "morahs" (chairs made out of beautifully crafted straw) and with "chicks" (roll-up screens made of thin reeds) .... again to keep out the sun and heat. I recall a lot of hysterics when one day the chick was unrolled and out flew some bats! Another constant feature of the verandah were the "chipcullies" (small lizards) who were always upside-down on the ceiling waiting to flick their long tongues out and catch the unsuspecting insect. Cruel children that we were, we discovered you could cut off the chipcullie's tail and it would still twitch for quite a while.

Daddy, Moyra, me and Mum with a tiny Toodles in her lap.

Even though the servants would clean every day, nothing could stop a thin layer of dust covering all the furniture and I recall how quickly the sky could turn from burning blue to black with the advent of a sandstorm and how the whirling, blinding sand could sting. Another kind of black cloud experienced, thankfully only once, was that of a storm of locusts ....horribly impressive.

My mother lost her wedding ring forever in the sand and Daddy was quite nervous till another one was purchased and placed upon her finger!

In contrast to taking cover from the sandstorms, we would run hysterically out into the rare rainfall to soothe our skins and get rid of our "prickly heat" (a red rash). The scent of the rain on the sand was magical and nourished a lovely tree with bright orange/red flowers which was called "Flame of the Forest".

Although there was electricity, I recall a servant sitting outside a room in the house of our neighbors, the Alwyns, pulling a cord which was attached to a large carpet hung horizontally from the ceiling in the adjacent room. This made the carpet flap and provide the inhabitants of the room with some breeze. Often though, the servant would tie the cord to his big toe and pump his foot to perform the job and this system worked well until he fell asleep! Hand-held "punkahs"(fans) were also operated by the servants.

Even though most Anglo Indians were by no means extremely well off, because labor was so cheap, most families could afford servants. The more servants, the more prestige….. and I believe the Viceroy of India in New Delhi, who was accorded hundreds of servants as befitted his high station, had one whose **only duty was to bring in the morning paper!**

We would enter through the archway at Madhargate to go to the bazaar where there were all manner of exotic crafts – intricately carved furniture, beautiful brassware, gorgeous fabrics, carpets, jewelry and a large variety of "choories" (bangles) from very inexpensive glass ones to expensive gold; all of which we took for granted then and wish I could possess now. Then there was "Lahore Confectioners" where we would stop as a special treat for delicious sweets. Of course there was the dust, the heat, the flies, the cows with the right-of-way, and the beggars but we were used to all that…….after all, we had never known anything else……..this was home.

The mosques and temples stood side by side and we would wake to the sound of the muezzin's cry of "Allah o akhbar" from the minaret of the mosque and the sounds of the Hindu temple bells. These two religions coexisted amicably till Mr. Jinnah came along, demanding autonomy for Muslims and the birth of a separate nation – Pakistan – and shouts of "Pakistan Zindabhad". People who had lived together for decades suddenly were killing each other and burning down each others' religious houses. I remember hearing the news of Gandhi's assassination and, young as I was, feeling the shockwaves of the nation. The Sikhs, warriors that they are, got full employment during these troubled times by being hired as bodyguards for both sides.

"Uncle" Dudley McMillan recounted horrendous stories of witnessing slaughter on the railways. He was an engine driver, as were many Anglo-Indians, and saw the blood of not only men but women and innocent children run red in the carriages as the trains were forcibly stopped and the killings began. These men were traumatized by the things they saw, the images never leaving their minds.

During the riots, the gates of Chisty Villas were locked and hordes of shouting, angry men rushed by with goods they had looted; then a sudden halt as a mirror was broken – the 7-year bad luck superstition apparently crossing cultures. (Another superstition was peacock feathers – we would never put them in the house as this was supposed to bring bad luck, the round circle in the design denoting the evil eye.)

One of our neighbors was a beautiful, young Muslim woman who was, according to her family's wishes, engaged to a suitable Muslim man. He was indeed, suitable in every way but was an albino with very pinkish skin and white hair and eyebrows and we wondered if that bothered her at all. In any case, the riots came between the betrothal and their wedding and they had to flee, leaving us wondering what fate lay in store for them and hoping they had escaped. "Inshallah" (God willing).

On the flat roof at Chisty Villas: Back row: Duncan Cruikshank, Norma Bray, Daphne Houston, Me, Judy Jean Louis, Daphne D'Silva & Eugene Blanchette. Front row: Christine D'Silva, Russell Blanchette, Gladys Cruikshank and Moyra.

Every Sunday we would have, more or less, the same beggars come to Chisty Villas for alms. We got to know them over the years and one in particular had our sympathy because he was a strong young man who was deaf and dumb. Then one day "Uncle" Eugene Blanchette was in the bazaar and to his consternation saw the young beggar gambling, laughing and yelling. Uncle got off his bike and confronted the fraud, asking how he could have taken money from us for all that time under false pretenses? The beggar just smiled and shrugged his shoulders contempt-uously – but, of course, he never came to Chisty Villas again.

Every so often families would put on their solar topees (pith helmets) and pile into whatever vehicle was available and go off for picnics. Favorite places were Happy Valley and Anasagah. Anasagah was set on a lake amidst beautiful gardens with white marble parapets done in lacy fretwork and domed pavillions in the style of the Taj Mahal.

My most vivid memory of Anasagah, however, was not of its beauty but of Joy Barron and her little dog. Coco. We were sitting by a parapet, enjoying the view and chatting, when Joy's little pup got excited, jumped up to catch a bird and went right over the parapet, falling about 30/40 ft into the lake. Joy screamed while we all leant over and craned our necks to locate the dog. Luckily, Coco was not injured, managed to swim to some steps and was deposited safely into sobbing Joy's arms.

Anasagah, just before Joy's dog fell into the lake

MY AYAH

Besides my sister and other children in the compound, my companion used to be Juni, one of the ayah's daughters, who was my age.

I recall crawling under the bed when we were about 7 years old and trying to smoke a "beeri" (Indian cigarette). I am glad to relate that experience turned me off smoking for the rest of my life!

The ayah was married to her second husband so he was known by the name "Cha Cha", which means uncle.

Me & Juni

We all got used to calling him by this name and one day my mother, my Aunt Dorothy, Joyce Pooler and I were in the bazaar doing some shopping. When it was time to go home, we looked around to hail a "tonga" (horse-drawn carriage) and were delighted when we spotted Cha Cha, who was a tonga-wallah, on the other side of the street. Without stopping to think, my mother, Joyce and Dorothy all yelled "Cha Cha, Cha Cha", much to the amusement of the Indians at the sight of these white ladies calling a tonga-man their uncle!

Another story connected to Cha Cha was when we hired him one rainy day to take us to Church. This involved going over Martindale Bridge which was quite steep. My mother and Aunt Dorothy were in the back seat and I was up front with Cha Cha (to make sure he did not use his whip!) when, because of the slippery conditions, the horse tripped and fell to his knees. Because of the gradient, he continued to slide and the carriage was now at a crazy angle with Mummy and Aunty way up in the air screaming their heads off while Cha Cha and I were practically on top of the horse's rear! Thankfully, Cha Cha was able to jump out fairly quickly and return things to normal – whereupon the hysterics turned into peals of relieved laughter.

Cha Cha, Ayah, Muni and Juni all used to live in one small room in the servants' quarters. They would whitewash it inside and out and decorate the walls in floral designs with colored paints. They would cook their food outside and use patties made of dried cow-dung for fuel.

What savings they had they wore on their body in the form of bangles, anklets, earrings and necklaces. This jewelry translated into dowries when their daughters got married – a more visible form of banking than money stuffed under the mattress. They were (as was the custom) in debt to the local "bunya" (merchant) and paid his usurious rate quite philosophically. It was just an early, less sophisticated form of the credit card system.

Me, Ayah, Daphne D'Silva & Toodles

Much later, when I was living in the U.S., through the kind assistance of friend and priest, Father Roger (Podgy) Lesser, I decided to get her out of debt by paying off the bunya and really quite upset her. She would rather have had the cash!

My most vivid remembrance of Cha Cha, however, was the time I went to see my beloved Ayah in her quarters and found him beating her. I remember laying into him with all my little might, kicking and screaming at him, till Ayah held me in her arms and stopped my sobbing. I never looked at Cha Cha the same way after that day.

Every year, Ayah used to go to Pushka to worship and I would cry and hold on to her sari and beg her not to go because there were crocodiles in the lake and we would hear of people being attacked. But she would laugh and assure me she would be all right and, thank goodness, she always returned safely.

My ayah was bitten by a scorpion one day and I remember her "cure". She took some metal "chaabies" (keys) and dragged one from the bite spot out towards her toes, flicking the poison out. I guess because she believed in it, the cure worked. Mind over matter……and there is a lot of evidence in India of that phenomenon. One can see "sadhus" (holy men) covered in ashes, metal sticks poking through both cheeks with no blood loss or apparent discomfort. Walking over coals and levitation are common sights. Shirley MacLaine records in her book "Don't Fall Off The Mountain" how, when she was very cold in the Himalayas, she was able to warm herself by mentally thinking of heat until she was actually perspiring.

The "metha" and "methrani" (the sweeper and his wife) used to do the dirty work such as cleaning out the bathrooms. They were of the "untouchable" class. Their little son was very keen to learn English and I would write the alphabet in the sand and try to teach the little "chokra" (boy) as much as I could.

Ayah used to take care of us and we had a "khansama" (cook) who prepared the food. Like all the "memsahibs" (ladies) my mother had a key ring which held the keys to various things. One of these was the "godown" (pantry) where the dry goods like rice, dhal (lentils), etc were kept. The cook would make a list of supplies and my mother would open the godown and distribute the items requested and then carefully turn the key in the big lock on the door. On payday, Mummy used to dole out the money and the servants would put their thumbprints on their account page in lieu of a signature, then put their hands together and touch their foreheads in the traditional "namaste".

The "dhobi" (washerman) would come to the house and pick up our dirty laundry. Mummy would tick off the items on a list and he would eventually bring back the clean, crisp, pressed items, having taken them down to the river, bashed them on a large stone, dried them in the sun and ironed them with an iron containing hot coals.

The "doodh-wallah" (milkman) used to bring his cow to the back door and milk her in front of my mother after first turning the vessel upside down to assure her there was no water in it. Then after the milk was in the vessel she would insert a hydrometer to ascertain its cream content,

The doodh-wallah gets into the picture

My father always disliked the way servants were generally treated – always suspiciously and with the foregone conclusion that they would rob you blind. He always left his change on the chest of drawers as a sign of trust and respect for our servants and I believe he was repaid in kind.

Once a pair of his white pants went missing and my mother was sure it was the "mali" (gardener) as he was the same size as my father. I remember Daddy saying "Well, he probably needs them more than I do".

Some people used to abuse their servants terribly, both verbally and physically, but I am proud to say (apart from my teasing the Ayah unmercifully) we treated our servants very well so they stayed with us.

CUISINE

The food we ate was an interesting combination of Indian and English cuisines with items like cutlets and stews, "moli", pepper water, poppadums, chapatti (Indian flat bread), dahl (lentil), rumble-tumble (scrambled eggs with finely chopped onions and green chilies), etc. When we weren't feeling too well, we would be fed kitcherie or pish-pash – a soupy rice dish which was nourishing and easy to digest. There was often a satisfying plate of curry and rice – still regarded by me as the best meal one can have. It is also well known that once some "burrah sahibs" (important gentlemen) returned from Poona and other stations abroad to the damp of Tunbridge Wells and various towns in England, they sorely missed their plate of curry and rice. Now, judging by the number of restaurants all over the country, most of England is addicted to Indian "*khana*" (food).

If one wants to be a vegetarian, the easiest way is to choose Indian cuisine. There are so many tasty vegetable dishes one hardly notices the absence of meat. The Hindus are very particular about food left over from someone else and will not eat it. They call it "*jootha*".

It is also a myth that all Indian food is very spicy and hot. Of course there are specific dishes like vindaloo and pahl that can make one drip with perspiration but the cuisine from north to south and east to west is so varied, one can take one's pick. Though he had lived in India for most of his life, my father could not tolerate spicy food whereas both I and my daughter Tina (who has never set foot on the sub-continent) will reach for the crushed chili before even tasting our food! And the best way to "put out the fire" is with "lussi", a drink made from thinned yogurt which can be served sweetened by fruit like mangoes.

Lunch and tea and dinner were served upper-class English-style with finger bowls, serviettes, properly laid china and cutlery. Mummy used to ring a small dinner bell and the servants used to serve and remove each course as completed, standing outside the dining room door, just out of sight.

Daddy always dressed for dinner, "pukkah sahib" (proper gentleman) that he was; indeed the English made rather a fetish of this practice. Even when they were traveling in the hinterlands attending to the business of the Empire and having to stay in "dak" bungalows in the middle of nowhere with only a servant for company, they would dress for dinner. Wouldn't want to go native, don't you know!

There was a utensil I have not seen since – slim like a pencil but scooped out down each end….one end slightly wider than the other. This implement was used to scoop the marrow out of any bones that might be incorporated in a dish. A marrowbone spoon! Very elegant.

Occasinally, a special treat was a small condensed milk can which we punctured with 2 holes and sucked out the sweet milky cream.

SCHOOL

The biggest involvements in our lives were the Roman Catholic Church, the Convent School and the Railway Institute.

Every Sunday we would either walk or take a tonga to St. Anselm's Cathedral for Mass along Srinagar Road, past the blindfolded bullock across from Chisty Villas who went round and round a contraption that ground seeds into oil, past the houses of the Millers and Auberts, over a small bridge spanning a large nullah (drainage canal), past the D'Sousas, the Gilberts and, opposite them, the home of my friend Philoo Prim and her uncle Dr. Prim's surgery, always careful to avoid any "poojas" (sacred offerings) in the roadway. Invariably we would stop at the small bazaar to watch the sweetmeat man make jalabees, ludoos, gulabjamuns and doodh-peras then continue past a small Hindu temple and a large dry goods store called Agrawals before reaching Martindale Bridge with the Anglican Church on the right. Some of the Anglo–Indians were Church of England but most, like my parents, were devout R.Cs.

St. Mary of the Angels Convent was run by French nuns of the Franciscan order. The convent itself was a massive building made of stone in the shape of a square with a garden inside and long corridors. The chapel (in the obligatory shape of the cross) was at one end, the nun's quarters along one side and the classrooms and dormitory along the others.

We all had to wear uniforms (white blouse, navy pinafore, hat) and which I firmly believe should be *de rigueur* in all schools everywhere. We were taught in "standards" (grades) until we reached the Senior Cambridge level when the "tests" (written exams) were sent to England to be "marked" (graded) by the professors at Cambridge University in England. It was torture waiting for the results as they were sent and returned via sea mail, which took months in those days. We waited anxiously for the arrival of the mailman with these "chitties" (letters).

We **always** stood when the teacher entered the class, **always** said "Good morning". It would not have occurred to us to show disrespect even when the teacher was a lay person but we weren't incapable of playing tricks in class at the risk of having a dunce cap placed on our heads and being ordered to stand in the corner. I recall dipping the ends of the Indian girls long braids (we used to call them plaits) into the ink wells. Their hair was always jet black so they never found out until they washed it! I would also surreptitiously tie their braids to the back of the bench so when the teacher asked them a question their heads would jerk back as they stood up!

If it was a really serious infraction, the teacher would march us up one of the long corridors, past all the other classrooms, to the Reverend Mother's office for a good talking to and maybe a caning on the palms of our hands. Oh the shame of it all! – and then, of course, we would have to face our parents' displeasure when the report got home.

It was an extremely good education, with the emphasis on academics. We had 10 subjects to conquer, the teachers moved from class to class (not the students) with weekly tests and report cards that had to be parentally signed and brought back every Monday.

In addition, at the end of each month, we'd have to congregate in the big hall. Mother Superior would sweep in, we'd all stand and lilt, "Good Morning, Reverend Mother", and she would seat herself on the raised dais with teachers on both sides. We would have to walk up to the dais and she would then give each student in the entire assembly her report card. One cringed at disappointing marks being revealed in this public forum.

Also, because of her French accent, every time she said, "surely" in a sentence I would jump, thinking she had said "Shirley"!

We were extremely well-grounded in history and geography and recall that one of the tasks was to be able to draw (freehand and without looking) a map of the world. It did not have to be detailed but that exercise left us all with a clear idea of where people lived geographically for the rest of our lives. This would be a good exercise especially for today's over-privileged Western children who have no idea where or how the rest of the world lives.

In the summer the nuns wore mostly white, with black additions on their wimples for more formal occasions. I loved their winter habits when they changed to a warmer cream and red.

On schooldays the ayah used to walk the mile or so from our house to the convent in the midday heat to bring me my lunch. We had a large covered shed by the playing fields with refectory tables and benches for this purpose. She would carry the food in a "tiffin-carrier", a really neat device still much in use in India. It consists of three or four round metal containers which fit on top each other and are held together by a handle that slots through side hooks on each bowl. The bottom bowl can be filled with hot water, thus keeping the food in upper carriers warm.

I am ashamed to relate I used to say, "Nyhee mangtah" (I don't want it) after ayah's long walk in the hot sun and her begging me to eat just a little. "Please, Shirley Babee, "thora, thora" (a little).

Outside the convent gate stood a vendor with a wooden cart on which there were all kinds of bottles filled with mysterious stuff. We were not supposed to go outside the gates but he used to have two things I craved. One was "churan", little black balls of goodness-knows-what, which were supposed to be good for one's digestion. The other was shaved ice. This was made by putting a piece of cloth over a small block of ice and scraping it against a steel blade set in a piece of wood. Then the shaved ice was formed into a ball, put on top of a paper cone and from an array of bottles he would pour sweet syrups over the ice in the most vivid of colors......red, orange, green, blue, and "gulabi" pink! I think these items immunized me for life!

After lunch, we R.Cs. would have to go into chapel for Rosary and a sermon. Some of us would sit on one side of the altar, facing the others on the opposite side and would start a yawn and see how far it would travel! We also had a priest who used to punctuate his words with "ah" and we would count how many times he would do this in the course of his sermon. You'd think we were not very pious but, in actual fact, we were caught up in the adoration of Baby Jesus and of the Holy Virgin.

Our priest, whose name was Father Bonaventure, was very tall and gaunt and dressed in the brown robe and sandals of the Franciscan order and looked the very image of Jesus. I have often thought that the present Roman Catholic Church would get a lot more converts if the Pope looked like that rather than robed in silken garments and ruby ring.

Spiritual Retreats were another way of serving God. At least twice a year we would have a retreat for a week or so. This consisted of no talking, so we wrote notes to each other till the nuns said that we were missing the point......the intent was to concentrate on the spiritual! There was a lot of going to chapel and reading about the saints and confession and communion.

I chose big Saint Teresa of Avila (as opposed to little Saint Teresa) for my role model one year and read that she had put a stone in her shoe to suffer in the name of Jesus. I promptly did the same and limped all the way home.

The other big thing about the retreat was the General Confession…..this was a confession of not just the sins you had committed since your last confession but the sins you had committed your whole life! Mea culpa, mea culpa, mea maxima culpa!

I used to take piano lessons and hated them because firstly, it cut into recess time and, secondly, I used to get rapped on the knuckles with a baton when I made a mistake!

The nuns also used to make us do needlework and should a needle break, we were instructed to find a crack in the corridor pillars and insert the broken pieces so as not to injure the bare feet of the servants. Since I had no intention of wearing the big bloomers we were making, I would take an unconscionable time. "Where have you been?" the nun in charge would enquire irritably on my return. "I couldn't find a proper crack, Sister", I would prevaricate.

The boys of St. Anselm's School were rigorously kept apart from us pure little convent girls. They used to go to ridiculous lengths to achieve this goal…..even closing the boy's school a few days after the girl's school so that the boarders (who lived in other towns) would not travel together; which made it difficult for brothers and sisters to coordinate travel plans. All this separation made things extremely exciting of course. I remember Clem Jansen just riding by Chisty Villas on his bike and waving to me and the

Cletus Patrick Jansen

blush starting at my toes. He eventually gave me my first kiss!

I am happy to report that we have kept in touch through the years and had the pleasure of celebrating Clem's 65th birthday with him, his wife Sheila and family and friends in Leicester, England in 1999.

The three terrors — Clem Jansen, (who now lives in England), Mel Collie (who now lives in Canada) & Duncan Cruikshank (who now lives in Australia)

Bicycles were our favorite mode of transport. My mother and father both had bikes and one day Daddy suggested that my mother take me on the back of her vehicle when I was just a baby. She, being very nervous, demurred, whereupon

I asked, "Why, Mummy? Are you afraid I will dribble off?" much to everyone's amusement.

On another occasion, I was riding a bike without rubber handles on the handlebars and fell off. Frank Blake ran over to make sure I was unhurt, which I was, except for a bruise on my tummy in the shape of a perfect blue circle!

Robert Walker & me up a tree in Narzirabad.

TOODLES

One day a man came in from Nazirabad with a puppy for sale and tried to persuade my mother to buy it. My mother expressed doubts about it's breeding, whereupon I chirped up, "O, don't worry, Mummy, it's breathing, it's breathing!"

The end result was that we acquired this little black and white pup who was not supposed to grow very big. We called him "Toodles" but he grew into quite a large dog. We would ask visitors if they would like to meet him and call, "Toodles, Toodles"; he would enter and only when their faces registered surprise would we remember that his name really did not suit him at all.

Because of his size, he wasn't very swift and was always unsuccessful in catching mice. He would see one, struggle to his feet, lumber towards the mouse and, because of the stone floors, would skid into whichever piece of furniture the mouse was already under by this time. So, one day, when he proudly walked up with a dead mouse in his mouth, we showered him with praise. Then Daddy took us aside (so as not to hurt his feelings) and told us that he had seen the mouse in the alley already very dead! We never let Toodles know we knew.

Toodles also hated his bath and if he heard us rattle his chain he would disappear, so we would have to creep up on him and, after the ablutions, keep him chained up or he would deliberately go and roll in the sand. Then there would be a period of sulking with a deliberate turning away of his head from any conciliatory approach.

He was a sweet-natured dog and would wait faithfully on the wall of the D'Silva's home for me to return from school, taking my wrist in his mouth and slowly guiding me home.

He also assumed the task of guarding Chisty Villas. From the vantage point of the parapet on the flat roof, he would bark a warning to whomever entered the big gate. The natives got to know him and would cry out, "TOODALS, TOODALS – tique hai" (it's o.k.) but he would haul himself all the way down, satisfy himself that the intruder was indeed "tique hai", then climb the stairs back up to his perch and fling himself down with a very big sigh. We'd say, "You don't have to do this, you know, Toods" but he obviously felt it was important and that it was his job.

A grown-up Toodles with me & Moyra

Another lasting image of Toodles is of him actually drooling with anticipation whenever fudge was being cooked! Sweet dog with a sweet tooth.

Speaking of sweet tooths, my father would forgo the main meal in favor of dessert every time! My mother always complained that she could just **look** at a piece of chocolate and put on weight, whereas my Dad could eat a whole slab with no effect. A sweet man with a sweet tooth.

THE INSTITUTE

The Railway Institute was the focal point of social activities for the Anglo-Indian community. It was a lovely building set in impressive grounds at the bottom of Martindale Bridge. There were tennis courts, a bowling green, polo/soccer field, covered viewing stand, a rose garden, bicycle shed and terraced lawns. The building itself boasted a covered portico, indoor badminton courts, a large hall used for functions as well as showing movies, a bar, a billiard room and a lounge with comfortable leather chairs. The bar was large and well-appointed where the sahibs (white gentlemen) could have their "chota pegs" (small shots) of whisky. They were served by "bearers" (waiters) in white uniforms with red turbans. The memsahibs would be served the more ladylike "shandies" – beer mixed with lemonade.

My father and mother and their friends used to play tennis while the ayahs looked after us children on the lawns. My dad was a very graceful player; years later, when I was in a finals match for table tennis (which I lost) the newspaper article spent more print on my style than on the victory of my opponent, who was rightly incensed …and I thought, "I have Daddy to thank for that".

Dad is second from the left with his great mop of hair which he never lost - it just turned gray.

Elegant he was and a good player but he lacked the killer instinct. His was definitely the English view of sports - "It does not matter whether you win or lose but how you play the game". This in direct opposition to my adopted U.S.A. where one motto is "Show me someone who comes in second and I'll show you a loser!".

I had a propensity as a young child of crunching ice and so I was nicknamed "buruf-wallah" (ice person) by "Uncle" Walter Bartlett. He wasn't a blood relative but, out of courtesy, we children always addressed our elders as "aunty" and "uncle". It surprises me even now when I hear a small child address a grownup by their first name.

"Uncle" Norman Kelly used to quip, "There are only two kinds of relatives – blood relatives and bloody relatives!"

Besides badminton and tennis and bowls, the club would put on dances and fancy dress parties. The wooden dance floor would be sprinkled with a white chalk powder to make it easier to glide on, the piano tuned and the chairs moved against the walls of the room for space and better viewing.

The memsahibs would look very beautiful in the latest dress they had seen in a current magazine and which they had shown to the "derzi" (tailor) with orders to reproduce it. He would then take her measurements, let her select a fabric from his stock and, presto, within days would have an exact copy. He would sit cross-legged at his sewing machine in his open shop in the bazaar and create these garments with no effort at all. When I grew older, I would give him my orders and, while bicycling past his shop would say, in Hindi, "Jaldi, jaldi, (hurry), derzi. The dance is tomorrow" and he would smile and reply "Acha, acha (okay), don't worry, Missy Babee……….but I know the dance is not till Saturday!"

The shoemaker would do the same……come to the house, put your foot on a piece of paper so he could trace the outline and presto! a custom pair within days. I remember being taken to see "The Wizard of Oz" and being so absolutely petrified of the Wicked Witch of the North that my mother had to take me out of the cinema but not before I had registered Judy Garland's red shoes! No rest for Mum until the shoemaker had made me a pair of red "joothies" (shoes).

Every year the Institute would also have a fancy dress party for us children and I was dressed up as a bee, a penguin, Red Riding Hood, a Scottish highlander, among others but the one I remember most is the one as a Muslim princess.

42

Our landlord, Chisty, lent us a beautiful crimson velvet "salvar/kamiz" (pants and shirt) encrusted with precious stones, a gauzy gold "duputta" (scarf), curled up toe slippers and a gold & ruby ornament for my forehead. I think I won.

Behind the Railway Institute was the steel railway bridge under which ran the railway lines. The Railway Quarters were situated by the lines on Beawar Road and there lived my friends Judy Jean Louis (who was part French and who spent her holidays in the Seychelles) and Norma Bray. The Andrades, the Blanchettes, the Jones, the Cecils, the Collies and the Nelsons lived in a section known as Hazaribagh which also included Freeland Home where the bachelors used to live (as did my Dad) before they got caught!

Further down the road was the Railway Hospital where we would endure innumerable injections and vaccinations. Then came the homes of the Jansens, the Bartletts, the Mahons and the Millingtons, among others.

I am very pleased to say that though we are flung to the far corners of the former British Empire, many of us stay in touch and even visit in person despite the distances involved.

ANIMALS

Another indelible memory of the Institute was a fair on the grounds with rides and games and an elephant. I had some peanuts in my little hand for him but he chose to put his trunk around me and take the ice cream cone right out of my other hand! I was so upset, I turned and grabbed a long pair of legs in brown trousers that was my Dad – or so I thought till I looked up ......it was a stranger! A dreadful day for a little girl, as affirmed by the vivid recollection umpteen years later!

My mother related this story about a friend of hers unpacking a dress that had netting over the satin. Her intention was to catch fireflies and put them between the two fabrics and, under the night stars, be a beautiful sight. So she slipped the dress on when, to her horror, she felt something slithery on her shoulder. She froze and, unable to bear the feeling, just crushed the offender in her hand. That's one of the things about India. You have to learn to co-exist with all sorts of creatures; monkeys, snakes, scorpions, spiders, mongoose and all manners of "boochies" (creepy crawlies) and that is not counting the larger animals in the jungle! But, after all is said and done, one can't scream all the time so you either leave or get on with it!

Another story my mother related was of one of her sisters coming home and plopping herself down on a long chair which had a wooden frame but rattan seats. She could hear this steady slap, slap, slap but could not figure out where it was coming from. Finally, she got up and saw the head of a lizard above the rattan which his body had slipped through and it was his tail slapping as he tried to extricate himself! Her blood ran cold as she thought what might have happened had she sat all the way back in the chair.

One of the smallest but most deadly of snakes is the krait and one day when school cupboards were being spring-cleaned, there was one, cozily curled up with the books! The nuns had a "chowkidar" (guard) come and remove it.

There are a thousand and one stories like these. I have seen a mongoose and snake fight (the mongoose always wins) and snake charmers with their cobras were a common sight. I recall when we used to sleep in the garden on some hot sultry nights under mosquito nets, always checking under the bed for snakes before going to sleep. No guarantee they would not slide up later but, as with all creatures, they are more scared of us than we of them and (unlike mankind) invariably attack only when threatened.

A decoration that was almost *de rigueur* was the tiger skin on the floor of the drawing room, mouth open in a frozen roar with big teeth showing. Inevitably, there were pictures of some great hunter standing with his rifle, hand on hip and his foot on top of a magnificent animal which, even then, struck me as obscene. What possible glory was there in sitting in a "machan" (platform) with a terrified, bleating goat tied up below as bait and waiting for an unsuspecting tiger to appear in the clearing? Or having the natives beat the bush till you had cornered the beautiful animal and could shoot him from the safety of the top of an elephant? Young as I was and indoctrinated with the normality of these "shikars" (hunts), I was such a pain about them that I was cordially "uninvited" to go on any– which was just fine by me.

Monkeys, while charming, could also be a nuisance as they were destructive and noisy and thieves but they were tolerated – not least because one of the Hindu gods is Hanuman, the Monkey God.

Aunt Dorothy used to teach in a school called Oakgrove in the hill-station of Musoorie in the Himalayas. Sometimes, due to severe travel sickness, she would remain on the premises during holidays and observe the monkeys. They would have been watching the children during school term and now, with the playgrounds empty, would come down and imitate everything they had seen, push each other on the swings, use the slides and applaud each other. Aunt Doro said they were just delightful.

Aunt Doro was my father's youngest sister and had been a fixture in our lives as long as we could remember. She was a small, gentle person with the most generous of hearts and a sunny personality. She had been a spinster for as long as we had known her and we, with a combination of the callousness of youth and English reserve, had never thought to enquire why this was so.

The years went by until one day Tricia gently probed into that area and Aunty told her that she had, indeed, been very much in love once. He was a young medical doctor, practicing in Musoorie, when they met at a local dance. Ian Fitzgerald was his name and he courted the shy Dorothy for quite a while before she felt confident enough to return his affection. They did, in due course, get engaged and when he introduced her to his family they too fell in love with the sweet Dorothy.

They were very happy and looking forward to their marriage when, one rainy, cold night, a patient of Ian's insisted that he come out in the foul weather to attend to her. He did so, riding his horse through the nasty night and seeing to his demanding patient. He returned safely but had caught a very bad chill which then turned into pneumonia and he became very ill. He sent for Dorothy and she came to his bedside but only in time to see him die.

By this time in the narrative, both Dorothy and Tricia were in tears and Dorothy, in her gentle way, expressed the wish that we should never speak of it again.

Dear Aunt Doro died at the age of 99 but we comfort ourselves with the knowledge that she is, at long last, with her beloved Ian.

Dorothy Gifford

MELAS (FESTIVALS)

We children loved the festival of Holi which was celebrated with the spraying of colored water in different hues and the throwing of colored powders. We used to put on old, white clothes, get pumps (made on the order of a bicycle pump), fill them with colored water and try and spray everyone.

Many years later I took my mother back to India and the festival of Holi fell during our visit to Delhi but we were told under no circumstances to venture forth as it was too dangerous. The colored waters were now fast dyes and there was an element of drunkenness and danger to the festivities which seemed a real shame. So I sat and watched what I could of the "tamasha" (revelry) from the safety of my hotel window when I heard a knock on the door. The cleaning woman came in and gently marked my forehead with colored powder! We laughed and I did not feel so left out of the festivities.

Another festival which we looked forward to was Divali – the festival of lights. The Hindus would get tiny clay bowls, fill them with oil and roll some cotton into thin wicks with one end dipped in the oil. Then thousands of these little "chiraghs" were placed on the rooftops and along walls and the whole city was made magical by their tiny lights.

Then there was the Hindu festival where they take a statue of the god Kali (the one with many arms and painted black) and, with much clashing of cymbals and ceremony, sink her in a body of water.

The Muslim festival of Muhorram was very different. There was the loud, incessant sounds of drums in a steady beat, men dressed as tigers balancing on bamboo beams and mock-fighting and, generally, a more sinister feel.

In contrast, was the joyous feasting at the festival of Eid after the holy week of fasting during the Haj.

The other images that have stayed with me are those of native funerals. The Hindus cremate and parade the body down to the river's edge on a stretcher held high on the shoulders of the pall bearers. The body of a woman is draped in white and that of a man in red fabric. The one that really stands out in my memory is that of a holy man because he was strapped into a sitting position under the drape and there was much music and dancing and throwing of paise (Indian coins) as he was assured a place in Nirvana.

MOVIES

I was named Shirley because my mother stated that if the first-born was a boy she would do the honors but if it was a girl my father could name the baby. Well, on November 3rd, 1935 I came along and Daddy, along with thousands of other dads at the time, named his daughter after the adorable child-star Shirley Temple. Believe me, if you meet a lady named Shirley you invariably know her age range!

Even though India was a long way from Hollywood, its impact was powerful and that of Little Miss Goldilocks even more so. I had a full-size cardboard cut-out doll and all her paper dresses, which designs my mother used to have the derzi duplicate, down to the embroidery.

Going to the movies (actually, we never said "movies", we called them "pictures" or "flicks") was an exciting event even if we had to sit in the "charzies" (cheap seats) because we might be able to hold hands with a boy! And Dolly Nelson's fresh potato chips were another pleasure.

One day, we went to see some spectacular with my grandparents who had purchased some meat samosas (patties) to munch on. Granddad Ernie had just taken his first bite and was savoring the taste when Granny Maggie let out a small shriek, "Oh my goodness! I forgot. It's Friday today. You can't eat meat!" and I recall Granddad's disgusted expression as he replied, "Gosh, Maggie, why couldn't you have remembered **after I'd finished".**

Granddad Ernie & Granny Maggie

My mother had a wonderful collection of posters which I am sure would be collector's items today but unfortunately were lost forever.

ANECDOTES

When WW II broke out in Europe in 1939 I was just four. We were insulated from the horrors by the distance involved but I do remember for some strange reason that we had ersatz powdered eggs. Much to Tony Webster's amusement I preferred them over fresh eggs and loved powered egg omelet's. Maybe it was because Tony was in the Army that we got the stuff. He was engaged to Joy Pooler at the time and looked very handsome in his uniform.

The only other impact of the war I can remember is a funny incident; my mother used to make me kneel by my bed, say my prayers and add "And help England to win".

One night she heard me intone, "and help England to win the game"

"What game?" she asked

"Aren't they playing a football match?" came the innocent reply. So, smothering a smile, my mother tried to explain the real situation.

My mother used to give us great parties with themes. One was in the form of a restaurant with tables covered in checkered cloths, menus with prices, us dressed up as waitresses with aprons and a cashier's desk with play money. One little invitee walked in, looked at the menu and promptly started to leave.

"Where are you going?" we asked

"I'm going home to get some money" was the reply till we laughed and explained the program to her.

A game we used to play was "church". We would set up seats in rows as pews in the garden with an aisle leading to the altar and a pulpit. I would then give a sermon but the whole point was to publish the bans of marriage between us girls and boys. Little Frieda Huq hated this particular boy and as soon as we published their marriage bans, she would promptly walk out of the "church"! We would run after her, promising not to do it again and, as soon as she was seduced back into her seat, we would repeat the offence. Wicked!

The neem tree was used by the natives for various purposes but the most efficient was the method of breaking off a twig, chewing the end till it became shredded and then using it as a toothbrush. This was not only economically and ecologically sound but very effective, judging from their sparkling white teeth except when stained brown by chewing "paan" (ground beetlenut wrapped in a green leaf).

There was a lovely neem tree right in front of our house which had a bent branch on which we all used to swing and from which one day Michael Patrick Cody fell and broke his arm.

My ayah used to decorate the palms of her hands and bottom of her feet with "mendhi" leaves. By crushing them and making a paste, they exuded a red dye with which she used to make elaborate designs. Many years later this adornment was embraced by the West as it could be used as temporary tattoos.

The "tikka", that red spot in the middle of the forehead which so intrigues foreigners, is 1. a marriage sign. 2. the center from where all good flows 3. just a decoration. Sometimes these can get quite elaborate in design and also very expensive in the form of jewels.

The sari is, of course, the most famous of Indian costumes and, besides it's beauty, one of the most forgiving articles of clothing ever devised. Since it consists of just 6 yards of material and, as the trick is all in the draping with no pins or stitches, one can gain or lose weight with no alteration necessary. However, the fly in the ointment here is the "choli" (blouse) that accompanies the sari. This top, which is matched to the sari, is not only tightly fitted but shows a bare midriff, so there's the rub!

A mile or so behind Chisty Villas lay Mayo College. This prestigious learning establishment was for the young heirs to the principalities of Jaipur, Jhodpur and Udaipur, among others. The main building in red sandstone was the college itself and the surrounding mini-palaces were for each prince and his retinue, all set amongst beautiful formal gardens.

An outstanding feature in the grounds was a large relief map of India with the Himalayas tipped in white and the rivers painted blue. Extremely effective. I would see the princes playing polo on their beautiful Arabian horses on my way to school.

One year we took a train trip to Karachi, before Pakistan was created, to visit my dad's sister, Alice. She was married to Reginald Reynolds and they had one son, my cousin Hubert. My dad's other sister, Lydia, also lived with them in a large flat on the first floor of a building on Preedy Street.

We enjoyed lovely days on the silver shores of Clifton Beach along with Uncle Ted Baldwin, Aunt Sally and cousin Babs, forays into the bazaar on Elphinston Road and ice-cream at the K-Wality Restaurant which was just around the corner.

The flat had a balcony which overlooked the busy thoroughfare and we children would spend hours watching the interesting sights. One day, one of the many camel carts passed by. These vehicles had long, large beds loaded with goods. This particular day, the driver was balancing himself just behind the camel holding the reins loosely in his hand while he concentrated on the lunch in his tiffin-carrier, with the result that he lost his balance and fell off. The camel cart then ran over him.

Viewing this drama from the balcony, we let out horrified screams and my parents, who were in the dining room, just froze in terror, thinking, of course, that one of us had fallen over. When they could move and ascertain that we were alright, we all turned our attention to the poor camel driver. Thankfully, these vehicles have huge rubber tires and this cart was empty, so he was not badly injured.

GAMES

Cricket and soccer were the English passions which they passed down to the rest of us and field hockey was a game at which the Indians excelled and would often play without shoes.

I remember the M.C.C. Cricket Team (Marylebone Cricket Club) coming to India and sitting in the hot sun under my parasol with my grandfather watching them play. They were accorded the same adulation as today's rock stars.

Gilly-dunda was a game we played a lot. A four-inch piece of wood was sharpened at both ends (the gilly) so that when hit it would fly up; then we would have to send it as far as possible by hitting it with the dunda (stick).

We would play rounders, hop-scotch and marbles. I remember "Aunty" Val Blake having a lovely bowl full of colored marbles on a table in her living room.

Kite-flying was another diversion. We used to make a paste from finely ground glass and "atta" (flour) paste called "manja" and apply it to our string; then when there was a battle in the air, one kite would get cut, drifting away forever into the blue, while the victorious kite was reeled in, ready to challenge new kites another day.

We also had Sports Day at school, which I dreaded. We would put on our white shorts, shirts, socks and keds (plimsoles) which we had all probably bought at Bata's Shoe Store.

One sports day we had the honor of Bishop D'Mello attending. I was late arriving for a foot race in which I had been entered, with the result that the line-up had to wait while I changed into my keds. Eventually, off went the starting gun ... and I finished next to last! Whenever I met Bishop D'Mello after that, he never failed to tease me, saying, "My goodness, what with the hold up and everything, I thought we were really going to see something!" Even after he was elevated to Archbishop of Bombay, I was not spared!

Another amusing incident at St. Anselm's Cathedral took place during Benediction. The service involves the swinging of an incense-burner with live coals activating the incense. The priest had his back to the congregation, when the altar boy (I forget now who it was) got a little too enthusiastic with his swing with the result that a hot coal fell out. He then tried to retrieve it with his bare hands, which little performance had the congregation unsuccessfully stifling their laughter and the priest wondering what on earth was going on behind his back!

Saintly Shirley!

At 7 years, the Church regarded us as having reached the age of reason and so we were allowed to make our First Confession and our First Holy Communion. We were dressed all in white like miniature brides and it was a joyous yet solemn occasion. Around the age of 12 or so, we would make our Confirmation and having just seen the movie "Song of Bernadette" and utterly moved by Jennifer Jones performance, I chose Bernadette as my confirmation name. So technically I am "Shirley Mary Melita Bernadette Gifford-Pritchard"!

We were taught our Catechism and thoroughly versed in the intricacies of the theology of the Roman Catholic Church. We knew the difference between venial and mortal sins and the sins of omission and commission; that we could err in word, thought and deed and, just to drive the point home, we were told some awfully frightening stories of transgressions that led to dire consequences.

The story I remember with the utmost clarity is that of a little girl who lied and then died unexpectedly, before she had time to confess or say an act of contrition. So there she was, placed in a lovely white coffin by the altar with the requiem mass in full swing and everyone in tears, when there was a "Tap, Tap, Tap". At first no one knew where it was coming from but then it became obvious that it was coming from the closed coffin. So the lid was lifted and, to everyone's horror, there was the little girl with her tongue out – and the tongue was **black**! So we knew where she had gone because she lied.

These stories might have kept us on the straight and narrow but, let me tell you, they were the stuff of nightmares.

The other scary stories one heard in India were those about black magic. Diana Bristow told me about the time the seniors were at late study. They were allowed to do this without supervision in the classroom and at late hours. She said there was this girl from South India who suggested that instead of studying they take time out to do some table rapping. This consisted of spreading out the alphabet on a table and then holding up a pice (a coin which had a hole in the middle) and intoning, "Any spirit passing by take possession of this ring". Well, according to Diana, the pice started just quivering in mid-air, whereupon half the class fled in terror. Diana said she stayed on and that the girl asked the spirit questions which he answered by directing the pice to the correct letters in the alphabet.

It turned out that it was the spirit of a former boyfriend of the girl and he warned her that she should not have called him up. Diana said that after that episode, they might be walking down a school corridor, when her friend would suddenly freeze and say, "It's him". Eventually, she could not concentrate on her studies and had to leave school.

Diana Bristow & me

Another black magic story was about an English lady with blonde hair. One day a vendor came to the door and asked the lady, if he were to come back the next day, would she be so kind as to give him a lock of her hair. She saw no harm in this until her servant said to her, "No, no, memsahib, do not give him anything of your person. Please, please listen to me. Give him some hairs off this rug instead". So she gave the vendor some strands off a camel hair rug that was similar in color to her hair, just to humor her servant. Well, a few nights later the camel hair rug disappeared and the servant said, "See, memsahib, if you hadn't listened to me that would have happened to **you**!"

We were never sure if these stores were true but we weren't going to take any chances!

NAGPUR

One day, when I was about 15 years old, Daddy announced that we were being transferred to Nagpur, so everything was packed and sad farewells were spoken. The most difficult was saying goodbye to my ayah. I was almost as much her child as was Juni and, in addition, we had been her livelihood and being an ayah was all she knew. I remember all of us on Ajmer Railway Station and her crying as the train pulled out, holding on to my hand until the very last second.

Ayah, Moyra & me

That was the last time I saw my ayah – but she lives on forever in my heart

And even though I was very sad at leaving, I must confess my feelings were tinged with the excitement of the unknown.

We traveled by train, which is still my favorite form of transportation. The British had for their own purposes of trade and communications knit the sub-continent together with a wonderful network of rail and road systems. English became the common language not only for India (which has numerous languages – not just dialects) but also for the rest of the world.

A train journey in India took days with vastly differing scenery and as we left the dry land and chugged through fertile jungles, I even caught sight of a black leopard in the trees, his eyes lit green, mesmerized by the lights of the carriages.

There were 1st, 2nd and 3rd class carriages and as the railways were the principal mode of long distance travel on the sub-continent, the carriages in 3rd class were often overcrowded with people hanging on quite precariously. This rail system was named the B.B. & C.I., which stood for Bombay, Baroda & Central India Railway.

The steam train would whistle, chug and puff on the narrow gauge lines, stopping at stations along the way with vendors singing out "Paan, Beeri, Cigarette" for sale. They would also sing out, "Cha, garam cha" and there would be large kettles of hot "chai" (tea with "masala" (Indian spices), boiled with the milk and sugar already added) bubbling on the platform.

Travelers could place an order for food at one station and when they arrived at a station around the time for lunch or dinner, there would appear a "thali", the message having been sent by Morse code. The thali, a round platter with divisions, had items such as rice, dhal, vegetable bujia, chappati and maybe a little raitha. Delicious!

Of course, as "whites" we did not order these thalis but had thermoses of tea and sandwiches and fruit which had been packed especially for the journey and which were replenished as needed.

Here I am inserting another of my mother's anecdotes about a train journey she took during her childhood:

SOLOMON'S FOLLY
by Lilian Giffford

"Hold baby, Solomon."

"Yes, Missy."

We were leaving our up-country home for a four-months' holiday "down south" -my two sisters, baby brother, Mummy and I. Accompanying us, after a three-year sojourn in the north, was our Tamil servant, Solomon. He had left his home a mere lad of 14 summers and was returning a man of 17!

Oh, what tales he would spin to his admiring relatives; how he would make them open their eyes in wonder at the marvels he had seen and the gifts he had bought them, now safely hidden in the bottom of his tin trunk. A beautifully chased brass mug for his father, a gay sari for his mother and, among other things, a tiny marble replica of the Taj Mahal for his uncle.

Nor had he neglected to purchase some finery for himself. Wouldn't the girls stare in admiration when they saw him in his new clothes, a brightly embroidered cap on his head! The last-named was for special occasions, "mela" (festival) days and such, but he also had a smart new brown one for everyday use.

A bell clanged, a whistle shrilled, the guard waved his flag; with a screech of brakes and a sudden lurch we were off! My mother settled back comfortably and held out her arms for my brother, George. Relieved of his task, Solomon streaked to the window next to ours, dropped the glass shutter and thrust his head out.

"Solomon, isn't that the new brown cap you are wearing?" asked my mother sharply.

Guiltily withdrawing his head from the window, he replied, "Yes, Missy"

"Why are you so foolish? Don't you know that it will become quite dirty by the time you reach home? Why don't you wear your old black one and change it just as we get to Madras?"

Solomon looked crestfallen. Gazing at Mummy with beseeching eyes, he pleaded, "But, Missy, I will be careful".

"Oh, well!," said my mother, relenting.

Grinning delightedly, Solomon once more turned to the window and looked out. Field upon field hurtled by. A few cows, grazing stolidly, lifted their heads to stare at the girl who was minding them. White teeth flashing, Solomon thrust his head father out to look at her. Pouf! A little round, brown object sailed away on the breeze, rolled a bit and came to rest in the middle of a field.

"Look, Mummy", we excitedly exclaimed, "Solomon's cap has flown away!"

"Well", said my mother sarcastically, "now all you have to do, Solomon, is to take out your embroidered one!".

Turning sheepishly, Solomon went to his box, opened it without a word and put on his old black cap.

Hour succeeded hour. We children were soon tired of staring out of the window at the monotonous flat countryside. Looking *for some diversion, we pounced on Solomon sitting glumly in his corner.*

"Come on, Solomon, sing to us."

Nothing loath, his face brightening, Solomon asked, "What song do you wish me to sing, Missy-baba?"

"Abie, Abie, My Boy, of course", we chorused.

Standing up and making a deep bow, Solomon began to sing in his high falsetto voice. Breathlessly we listened, waiting for the last line "Abie my boy, what are you waiting for now?" when, with a smirk, Solomon would end by whispering behind his hand, "Next pay day!" This never failed to amuse us and we clapped our hands and called for more.

Night fell, then began another day more monotonous than the first. Restless and fretful, we children harassed our poor mother and faithful servant.

We changed trains. As this was a fast mail and crowded, Solomon did not travel with us but in a third class compartment close to ours. Once more we fell to gazing out of the windows. Gone were the dun coloured plains of the north, giving place to vivid green paddy fields, rich red soil, topped by a dazzling blue sky. The names on the railway station boards began lengthening; the calls of vendors shrilled forth in a language strange to our ears, accustomed only to Hindi. Even the dress of the people was different.

After a time, my mother noticed that our "surai" (clay goblet) in its wooden travelling stand, was empty. Calling Solomon at the next halt, she handed it over, cautioning him to fill it at the next big station.

"Mind you don't try to fill it at a small station. This is a mail train and stops for just a minute or so at these."

Promising to be careful, Solomon retreated to his compartment with the empty surai. A lurch and we were off once more. About 20 minutes later the train pulled in at a small station. Solomon noticed a tap right in line with his carriage. Forgetting Mummy's instructions, he nipped out and began filling the surai. Hardly had he commenced when the guard's whistle shrilled and we moved off.

"Solomon!" we shrieked. Turning, Solomon ran and tried to regain his compartment. He was unable to make it. Leaning out of the window, my mother called out and made signs to him to jump into any other carriage. Solomon paid no heed. Terror-stricken, he had lost his head completely. The train gathered speed but still the boy kept running.

The guard was standing in the doorway of his van next to ours. My mother called out to him, begging him to stop the train, but he ignored her frantic plea.

In the meantime, we had thundered out of the station yard and crossed a small bridge just outside. Horror-stricken, we saw Solomon gain the bridge and try to cross it. This was too much for my mother. Terrified lest he should miss his step and plunge between the widely spaced planks of the bridge, she turned and wrenched at the emergency cord. It was stiff. Desperately she tugged again.... there was a sudden jolt, a screech of brakes and the train came to an abrupt halt. We had stopped on a curve and our "bogey" (compartment) being in the middle of the train, heads popped out of windows on each side of us, curious to know what was wrong. Furious and red-faced, the guard came up to our carriage with its tell-tale arm sticking out of the roof.

Confronting my mother, he said sternly, "Do you know, madam, that you will have to pay a 50 rupee fine for this?"

Inwardly quaking (as she informed us afterwards), my mother put on a bold front and answered, "You may make your report at destination and I will make mine. I did not pull the chain before appealing to you but you ignored my request even though you saw that the boy might have dropped to his death."

Just then Solomon came up panting and fell at my mother's feet. Holding up the surai that he still clutched in one hand, he jerked out, "Missy, Missy, but I did not break the surai!"

This surprising statement left my mother speechless for the moment. Recovering and flushing with temper she said bitterly, "Oh, Solomon, you stupid boy! You talk about saving a two-pice surai when I shall have to pay a 50 rupee fine on account of your foolishness."

However, seeing that he was in no condition for a scolding and secretly glad to have him safe once more, my mother said no more (for the moment!) but set about reviving him.

In the meantime, the guard had been busy. A long pole was procured, some mysterious rite performed and the jutting arm overhead disappeared. The engine whistled, the train jerked, heads were pulled in from the windows and we were once more on our way.

The rest of the journey was uneventful, but we noticed the guard would not look at us each time he had occasion to pass our window. Perhaps he was ashamed of himself or else felt sorry for my mother - who knows? At any rate no complaint was made at destination and my mother never had to pay the fine, much to her relief.

Solomon has grown old in the service of our family. He still sings "Abie, My Boy" but now it is to amuse my children. Sometimes we tease him and recall to his mind the incidents of the cap and surai, affectionately referred to by the family as **"Solomon's Folly".**

There was a scare at a station where we had to change trains. We saw Toodles being led away on the platform and thought they might have put him on the wrong train and that we would never see him again .. but when we rolled into Nagpur we were overjoyed to see he had arrived safely.

Nagpur is situated almost slap-bang in the middle of India. This town, unlike Ajmer, has no water shortage as the monsoon hits approximately a fortnight after it crosses the Western Ghats, having already poured torrents in Bombay. At times the downpour is so dense, one cannot see through the sheets of falling water. It was very disturbing for us, who were so used to conserving every drop, to hear the sound of water running wastefully away.

Nagpur is famous for its oranges, which are exported all over India. Papayas, guavas, custard apples, melons, plantains and plums were also enjoyed but the fruit which is absolutely delicious and has many varieties in India is the mango. There are the sucking kind, small with a very thin skin and so juicy they are best eaten with ones elbows in a basin of water! The Alphonso, a great "cutting" mango, and the "katcha" (green) mangoes which were boiled with milk and sugar and made into "mango phul". This drink, served very cold over ice, was like nectar on hot nights.

*I must recount here an incident regarding this drink. Many, many years later we were at an Indian restaurant in Westlake Village, California and my sister Moyra asked the waitress, "Can I have some mango phul" whereupon her Irish husband, Brian, who was very witty, turned to her and said, "That was pretty rude. How would you like it if she replied, "I don't have any, stupid!" Well, we all cracked up at this witticism, were still giggling when the waitress returned and Brian enquired, "May I have some kulfi" (a milky Indian dessert) and which she misheard as "coffee". She asked, "Do you want black or white?" and Brian's face was a picture as he turned to Moyra and asked, "There's **black** kulfi?". Well, that took us right over the edge!*

Roman Catholic Cathedral in Nagpur

We settled into a house on Kamptee Road across from the Cathedral and the Catholic Club. We shared this house, which had a large garden and a big gate, with the Menezes family.

Every Sunday I would go to the gate to give the beggars some coins and one in particular is scorched into my memory; she was little girl who was a leper, carried by her blind father; so she was his eyes and he her legs. Enough to break your heart. She would put out her little hand for the coins and I had to be careful as her fingers were already gone and, one day, in the attempt not to let the coins fall, I actually touched her hand. I remember going back to the house in a panic and scrubbing myself with Dettol (antiseptic) because I was so afraid I would catch leprosy.

One of the most distressing things about India and other third world countries is the poverty, especially poignant when it affects children. The difference between the have and have-nots is most evident at this the start of the 21st century and will have to be addressed, one way or another. As Gandhiji said, "The worst violence of all is poverty" .

So, life settled down into more or less the same pattern as in Ajmer between school, church and club. This time it was St. Joseph's Convent for us R.C's. and Bishop Cotton for the C. of E's. (Church of England).

However, there was one major difference….my mother's sister Thelma had become a nun (Sister Margaret Mary) and was one of my teachers! This was not good. Even _more_ direct input than the dreaded report card and, though she tried to stay impartial, if I had done badly in a test I could always tell from the color of her eyes….which would change from their normal gray blue to green!

*The glamorous Thelma
before taking her vows*　　　　　　*As Sister Margaret Mary*

There were the usual retreats with silence, confession, communion and reflection on the lives of the saints whom we would, hopefully, emulate. Again, the General Confession was on the agenda and sinners that we were, we had to write down this long litany of offences. Marie Lobo was in front of me in the confessional line when she turned towards me in a panic and whispered. "I've lost my list!" Holy horrors! She had a most distinguishable handwriting, so we prowled the corridors until, to her immense relief, we found the scrap of paper. I think back now of how innocent we were and what innocuous stuff must have been on those lists!

One of the Indian girls in the class was Kalpana Gupta, a chubby, sweet-natured girl from Bengal, who used to study everything by rote. She would sway back and forth in her seat and learn every lesson word for word - which was fine except when she forgot a word - then the whole system would crash! I, on the other hand, was prone to day-dream, looking out of the window at a big tamarind tree until reprimanded.

We would play field hockey on the "maidan" (open field) opposite the convent, netball in the quadrangle and suffer through P.E. in the big hall. I would walk home in the heat carrying my satchel (sometimes through the "busthees" as it was quicker) and arrive home perspiring, shoes all dusty to be greeted with a lovely tea. Once an Indian boy offered to take me home on the crossbar of his bicycle and I was too shy and embarrassed to decline. I got a good talking to when I got home – partly because he was a boy and partly because he was Indian.

We had an official tuck-shop (sweets and things) and the tuck man had a little building just inside the gates so it was felt his stuff was sanitary and therefore safe. Well, just outside the back gate sat a vendor with "salty beroes". These were plums that were boiled with "jaggery" (molasses) till they were soft and sweet, then sprinkled with hot red chili powder and salt. I loved those things and would forgo the tuck shop and risk sneaking out the back gate for the salty beroes.

A few years later I had the opportunity to return to India as I was working for Air India on Bond Street in London. When I got back to Nagpur, I went to visit the Lobo twins, Marie and Cynthia, at their home in Mohan Nagar, which was right by the convent. So naturally I said I wanted to go see the salty beroe man and, sure enough, there he was, just as I had left him, but for the first time I consciously registered the "gunny sack" (jute bag), the dust, and the flies. However, there was no way I wasn't going to support him and yes, they tasted just as good as ever!

In Clark Town lived my best friend, Diana Higher, whose mother, Daphne had been my mother's best friend when they were young. Also in Clark Town lived another friend, Cynthia Fowler, her mother and sisters and her cousins, the De la Hoyds. The Joseph family made up a large part of our "gang". Then there were the O'dea's, the DaCostas, the Vaz family, the Thompsetts, the Johnsons, the Lawries, at least 2 sets of D'Souzas, at least 3 sets of Fernandes, and, of course, the Lobo twins, among others.

There were three Shirleys in this remote town of India -Shirley Joseph, Shirley Stevens and myself – affirming my comment on the influence of Little Miss Temple.

There was also a Sherley Sylvester – but he was a boy.

Diana & I, posed and photographed by Mervyn Rodericks

So life continued much as before despite the change in location....only now we were teenagers and growing up. There were socials and dances but our parents were always in evidence at these functions, which had the same effect as being chaperoned. We were all very shy and the boys rather awkward and I remember my Dad dancing with me and each of my friends in turn so no one would be a wallflower, giving us confidence should a boy have enough courage to cross the floor and ask us. Very soon we sorted out our favorites and it was known that so-and-so was so-and-so's girlfriend or boyfriend. However, if we danced too many dances with one particular boy, we were soon reprimanded by our ever-present parents. Consequently the last dance became very important....that was the one you had with the favored choice.....but not too close or there would be trouble!

Shirley Jo & Earle, myself & Ronnie, Diana & No

Then came the day for my first long dance dress, which was really my mother's choice. It was white with little gold flowers sprinkled all over and puff sleeves. I think it was tall Cyril Fernandez who teased while whirling me around the floor, "Shirley, you look lovely but this looks more like a christening robe than your first ball gown!"

Picnics were big on the agenda and Telenkeri, which had a lake and lovely gardens, was a favorite. Picnics by moonlight were common during hot summer nights. My mother recalled moonlight picnics on the grounds of the Taj Mahal when the family was stationed in Agra. Now, of course, security concerns close the grounds at night.

There were more bicycle rickshaws than in Ajmer and it was difficult to watch those skinny, sinewy legs of the poor rickshaw man straining away in front; so when motorized rickshaws came in, it was a relief for all concerned.

We used to go shopping in Sadar Bazaar and be amused at the language the shopkeepers had innocently picked up from the Tommies (English non- commissioned soldiers). "Salaam, memsahib, damn nice shoes," or "Buy, buy, madam. This is bloody good" .... much to the memsahibs' disapproval!

We learned to call each other "guddhas" (donkey) as a mild insult but knew never to call a Muslim a "sooer ke buthca" (son of a pig) because that was a most serious insult.

"The gang" at a party in Nagpur

The Anglo-Indian community, though comparatively small and spread throughout the length and breadth of India, was very close because of the nature of their employment. They were constantly being transferred and so, even if you did not know a family personally, you would know about them

*Daddy in his solar topee
(pith hat)*

Nagpur, being a major stop between Calcutta and Bombay, had a big railway station and Daddy was always calling up the station-master to find out the time of arrival because people were either arriving, departing or passing through......and the train was **never** *on time.*

One day, Daddy called and was informed the train was due.

"My goodness, Station-master", exclaimed my father, "Are you telling me the Bombay train is on time?"

"Jee Ha (Yes), Sahib," came the reply "It is most definitely on time ....but it is yesterday's train"!

Years later I took my mother back to India and we found ourselves on Nagpur Station waiting for the very same train – and yes, it was 6 hours behind schedule! That's why we use the expression "Indian Standard Time" – meaning one will be late!

We all sat for our Senior Cambridge Examination with fear and trembling, and during the long interim of waiting for the results our parents sent us girls (not the boys!) off to learn shorthand and typing. But eventually the good news arrived that we had all passed and were now proud possessors of University Of Cambridge Senior Certificates.

In the meanwhile, the exodus from India by the English was complete, the word "posh" having been compiled by their experience of coming out to India and going home to England. It was "**p**ortside **o**ut" – "**s**tarboard **h**ome".

They had been followed by waves upon waves of Anglo-Indians who now belonged nowhere. My parents held on till

1952 and then made the difficult decision to emigrate, more for the future of their three girls than for themselves.

One of the last pictures taken in India. Me, Mum, Baby Tricia

In those days, Australia was closed by their "whites only" policy to almost anyone from Asia, South Africa had a apartheid situation that might have viewed Anglo-Indians as "colored" and that we might end up on the "wrong side of the tracks", Canada was colder and further away – and so the majority opted for England, the Motherland.

Again, goodbyes were said on a railway platform and tears shed at leaving friends and family and goods and chattels packed into steel trunks and our names stenciled on in white paint. Toodles had died so we were spared that heartbreak but leaving Mummy's sister, Thelma (Sister Margaret Mary), my teacher, was wrenching.

Though again, I must admit, once the train had slowly pulled out of the station, my feelings were mixed; scared and at the same time excited at the start of this big adventure.

We arrived at the magnificent Victoria Station in Bombay where we spent a few days with my mother's brother, George Dorsey, his wife Doreen, their four children and Granny Maggie. Then all too soon it was time to board ship and this was an even more excruciating farewell for my mother.

The P. & O. liner "STRATHAID" slowly pulled out of Bombay Harbor and the family figures on the dock, waving tearfully, framed by the Gateway of India, slowly receded into oblivion leaving us wondering whether we would ever see them or the land of our birth again.

When they finally disappeared from view, we reluctantly turned our attention to the novelty and distractions of the voyage.

We sailed over the Arabian Sea, past Aden, stopping at Port Said. The ship then negotiated the Suez Canal and sailed into the Mediterranean, past the boot of Italy and an erupting Mount Etna. We docked at Marseille, then continued past Gibraltar and into a stormy Bay of Biscay.

We finally found ourselves at cold, damp Tilbury Docks on a rainy day in London. I was 18 years of age .... and so ended my childhood in India.

The Gateway of India

ABOUT THE AUTHOR

I have always loved communicating through the written word and, before the age of the computer, letter-writing was the means and a pleasure – both in the writing and the receiving.

Now e-mail makes the process much, much easier with the added convenience of sending the missive to multiple recipients with just the touch of a button. What is lost, of course, is lovely letter paper and individual and unique hand-written script.

This is my first book, which happened really by accident. When our mother died, my two sisters and I were sorting her possessions in her house in England and a lot of old black and white photographs came to light, almost demanding to be put in some semblance of order.

Once that was accomplished, it seemed imperative that the people in those images needed to be identified. Before I knew it, I was penning my fond memories of them and of my childhood.

I sincerely hope you will find the stories about my family & India of interest.

Shirley Gifford-Pritchard
e-mail: brianfpr@adelphia.net

Printed in Great Britain
by Amazon